Quick Knit Afghans

by Rita Weiss

Leisure Arts, Inc.,
Little Rock, Arkansas

Produced by

Production Team

Creative Directors: Jean Leinhauser and Rita Weiss
Senior Technical Editor: Ellen W. Liberles
Photographer: Carol Wilson Mansfield
Pattern Testers: Kimberly Britt, Carrie Cristiano, Patricia Honaker, Debra Hughes, and Wendy Meier
Book Design: Linda Causee

Published by Leisure Arts

© 2011 by Leisure Arts, Inc.,
5301 Ranch Drive
Little Rock, AR 72223
www.leisurearts.com

All rights reserved. This publication is protected under federal copyright laws. Reproduction or distribution of this publication or any other Leisure Arts publication, including publications which are out of print, is prohibited unless specifically authorized. This includes, but is not limited to, any form of reproduction or distribution on or through the Internet, including posting, scanning, or e-mail transmission.

Although we have made every effort to be sure that these instructions are accurate and complete, we are not responsible for any typographical errors, or mistakes, or for variations in the work of individuals.

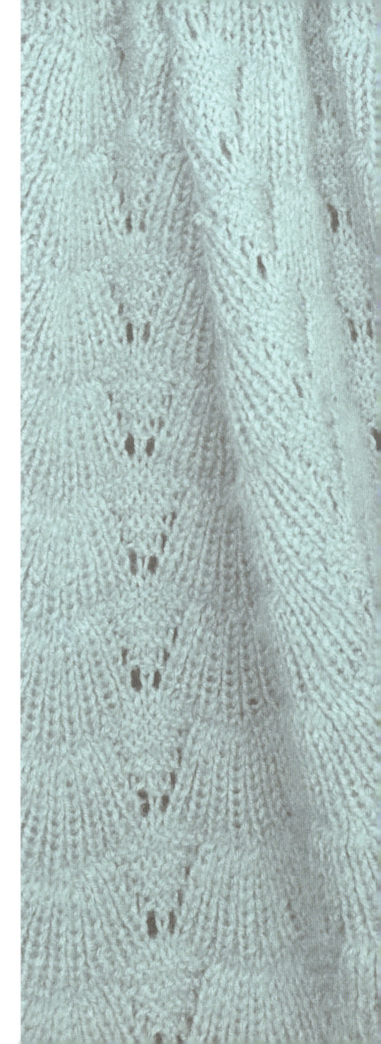

Introduction

We knitters are sometimes a bit reluctant to take on creating an entire afghan, worrying about how much time such a project might take. So we've created eight striking afghans that are fast and fun to make, and are perfect for gift giving because they'll find a welcome addition to any décor.

Big needles, multi-stranded yarn, easy stitches: these all add up to a fun, but not time-consuming adventure for knitters.

If you are a traditionalist who likes old favorite afghan patterns like ripples, try our Rapid Ripple made with two colors of bulky-weight yarn and size 13 (9 mm) knitting needles. It will be the fastest ripple you've ever knitted. Want something a little different? How about an afghan that resembles a patchwork quilt? Try Rosy Outlook made with two strands of two medium-weight yarns. Put two contrasting strands together to create a third color.

Here is an entire collection of quick afghan patterns to choose from. If, however, all you want to do is to knit without any thoughts to purling, or yarn overs, or bobbles, then just try Garter Greatness. Here you take two strands of two different color yarns, sit in your easy chair and using those four strands together, just knit until you have knitted enough to make a warm and cozy afghan.

So get out those knitting needles, gather together some yarn and start making some quick and easy afghans. You're going to have fun, and along the way you're going to make some wonderful afghans that will amaze your family and friends as well as yourself.

RAPID RIPPLE

Skill Level: Easy

Gentle waves are sparked with a bright red to add fire and excitement to this fun-to-make afghan. Using two strands of two different bulky weight yarns makes this afghan quick to make and especially warm for the lucky recipient.

Size
Approximately 40" x 56" (102 cm x 142 cm)

Materials
Bulky Weight yarn

[100% acrylic, 3.5 ounces, 138 yards (100 grams, 126 meters) per skein]

    6 balls red (color A)

    12 balls grey (Color B)

Note: *Photographed model made with Red Heart® Chunky™ #7252 Fire (Color A) and #7857 Coastal (Color B)*

36" size 13 (9 mm) circular knitting needle (or size required for gauge)

Gauge
12 sts= 5" (13 cm) with two strands in garter st (knit each row)

INSTRUCTIONS
With two strands of Color A, CO 108 sts; do not join, work back and forth in rows.

BOTTOM BORDER
Knit 5 rows. At end of last row, cut Color A; attach two strands of Color B.

BODY
Row 1 (right side): With two strands of B, knit.

Row 2: Purl.

Row 3: (K2tog) 3 times; *(YO, K1) 6 times, (K2tog) 6 times; rep from * to last 12 sts, (YO, K1) 6 times, (K2tog) 3 times.

Row 4: Knit.

Row 5: Rep Row 1.

Instructions continued on page 6.

Row 6: Rep Row 2.

Row 7: Rep Row 3.

Row 8: Rep Row 4.

Row 9: Rep Row 1.

Row 10: Rep Row 2.

Row 11: Rep Row 3.

Row 12: Rep Row 4.

Row 13: Rep Row 1.

Row 14: Rep Row 2.

Row 15: Rep Row 3.

Row 16: Rep Row 4.

Row 17: Rep Row 1.

Row 18: Rep Row 2. At end of Row 18, cut Color B and attach two strands of Color A.

Row 19: With 2 strands of Color A, rep Row 3.

Row 20: Rep Row 4.

Rows 21 through 24: Knit. At end of Row 24, cut Color A and attach two strands of Color B.

Repeat Rows 1 through 24 until the afghan measures approximately 56" (142 cm).

Southwest Landscape

Skill Level: Intermediate

A hint of the Southwest is echoed in this rich clay-colored lacy throw. By using a bulky weight yarn and large needles, you can knit this lovely throw in record time.

Size
Approximately 36" x 56" (91 cm x 142 cm)

Materials
Bulky Weight yarn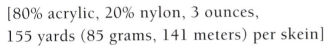

[80% acrylic, 20% nylon, 3 ounces, 155 yards (85 grams, 141 meters) per skein]

    7 balls rust

Note: *Photographed model made with Caron® Dazzleaire #0004 Clay Pot*

36" Size 10.5 (6.5 mm) knitting needle (or size required for gauge)

Gauge
12 sts = 4" (10 cm) in stockinette st (knit one row; purl one row)

Instructions continued on page 9

INSTRUCTIONS

CO 117 sts loosely. Do not join, work back and forth in rows.

Row 1: Knit across.

Row 2: Knit across.

Row 3: Knit across.

Row 4: Knit across.

Row 5: K5; *(K2tog) twice; (YO, K1) 3 times; YO, (sl 1, K1, PSSO) twice, K1; rep from * to last 4 sts, K4.

Row 6: K4, purl to last 4 sts, K4.

Row 7: K5; *(K2tog) twice; (YO, K1) 3 times; YO, (sl 1, K1, PSSO) twice, K1; rep from * to last 4 sts, K4.

Row 8: K4, purl to last 4 sts, K4.

Row 9: K5; *(K2tog) twice; (YO, K1) 3 times; YO, (sl 1, K1, PSSO) twice, K1; rep from * to last 4 sts, K4.

Row 10: K4, purl to last 4 sts, K4.

Row 11: K5; *(K2tog) twice; (YO, K1) 3 times; YO, (sl 1, K1, PSSO) twice, K1; rep from * to last 4 sts, K4.

Row 12: K4, purl to last 4 sts, K4.

Repeat Rows 1 through 12 until afghan measures approximately 54". Knit 6 more rows. BO all sts loosely. Weave in all ends.

ROSY OUTLOOK
Skill Level: Easy

An afghan that looks like a patchwork quilt combines rosy shades to accent any room. The quilt squares are made with a dark magenta yarn, a light pink yarn and a combination of both colors all worked together in strips.

Size

Approximately: 48" x 56" (122 cm x 142 cm)

Materials

Medium Weight yarn

[100% acrylic, 7 ounces, 364 yards (198 grams, 333 meters) per skein]

    4 skeins magenta (Color A)

    3 skeins pink (Color B)

Note: *Photographed model made with Red Heart® Super Saver® #905 Magenta (Color A) and #372 Rose Pink (Color B)*

Size 17 (12.75 mm) knitting needles (or size required for gauge)

Yarn needle

Stitch Guide

YF: with yarn in front as to purl

YB: with yarn in back as to knit

Gauge

10 sts = 4" (10 cm) with 2 strands of yarn in pattern

Pattern

Row 1 (wrong side): *K1, YF, sl 1 as to purl, YB; rep from * to last st, K1.

Row 2 (right side): K1, P1; *YB, sl 1 as to purl, YF, P1; rep from * to last st, K1.

Repeat Rows 1 and 2 for pattern.

Instructions continued on page 12

INSTRUCTIONS

Note: *Yarn is used double throughout.*

Strip 1 (Make 4)

With 2 strands of Color A, CO 17 sts. Work 22 rows of each of the following color combinations following the pattern stitch instructions:

2 strands Color A

1 strand each Color A and Color B

2 strands Color B

1 strand each color A and Color B

2 strands Color A

1 strand each Color A and Color B

2 strands Color B

1 strand each Color A and Color B

2 strands Color A

At end of strip, BO all sts. Weave in all ends.

Strip 2 (Make 3)

With 2 strands of Color B, CO 17 sts. Work 22 rows of each of the following color combinations following the pattern stitch instructions:

2 strands Color B

1 strand each Color B and Color A

2 strands Color A

1 strand each Color B and Color A

2 strands color B

1 strand each Color B and Color A

2 strands Color A

1 strand each Color B and Color A

2 strands color B

At end of strip, BO all sts. Weave in all ends.

ASSEMBLING

Arrange strips side by side with Strip 1 and Strip 2 alternating, making certain that the CO edge of each strip is at the same edge of the afghan. Sew the strips together with Color A, carefully matching the rows. Weave in all ends.

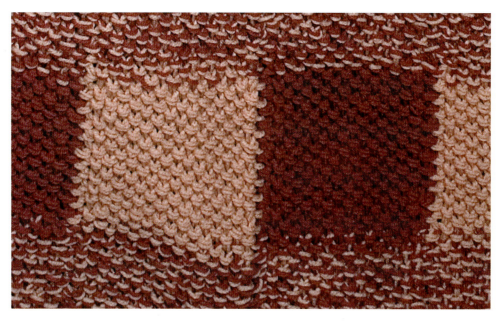

Sweet Honeycomb

Skill Level: Easy

A fun-to-knit textured stitch shows off to perfection in gleaming white. Two strands of medium weight yarn on a large needle will make this afghan quick and easy. Finish it off with triple knot fringe for that added touch.

Size
Approximately 48" x 60" (122 cm x 152 cm)

Materials
Medium Weight yarn

[100% acrylic, 7 ounces, 364 yards (198 grams, 333 meters) per skein]

    10 skeins white

Note: *Photographed model made with Red Heart® Super Saver® #311 white*

36" size 13 (9 mm) circular knitting needle (or size required for gauge)

Gauge
11 sts= 3" (28 cm) with 2 strands of yarn in pattern

Pattern
Row 1: Purl.

Row 2: K2tog; *(K1, YO, K1) in next st, sl 1 as to purl, K2tog, PSSO; rep from * to last 3 sts; (K1, YO, K1) in next st, sl 1 as to purl, K1, PSSO.

Repeat Rows 1 and 2 for pattern.

Instructions continued on page 15

INSTRUCTIONS

Note: *Yarn is used double throughout.*

With 2 strands of yarn, CO 177 sts loosely, Do not join; work back and forth in rows.

Row 1 (wrong side): Purl.

Row 2: K2tog; *(K1, YO, K1) in next st, sl 1 as to purl, K2tog, PSSO; rep from * to last 3 sts; (K1, YO, K1) in next st, sl 1 as to purl, K1, PSSO.

Repeat Rows 1 and 2 until piece measures approximately 60" (152 cm), ending by working a Row 2.

BO loosely in purl; weave in all ends.

FRINGE

Following instructios on page 32, make Triple Knot Fringe. Cut strands 30" (76 cm); use 8 strands for each knot, Tie knot through every other cast-on or bound-off st across each short end of afghan. Trim ends evenly.

Dazzling Peacock

Skill Level: Intermediate

Flaming peacock tails combined with open work add up to a striking coverlet. Because it is made with bulky weight yarn, the afghan is quick to knit, but will be appreciated for years to come.

Size
Approximately 48" x 60" (122 cm x 152 cm)

Materials
Bulky Weight yarn

[80% acrylic, 20% nylon, 3 ounces, 155 yards (85 grams, 141 meters) per skein]

    11 balls green

Note: *Photographed model made with Caron® Dazzleaire #0005 Tidal Pool*

48" size 11 circular knitting needle (or size required for gauge)

Gauge
12 sts = 4" (10 cm) in stockinette st (knit one row; purl one row)

Instructions

CO 147 sts. Do not join; work back and forth in rows.

Note: *Rows 1, 2, 5 and 7 are each increased by 18 sts (72 sts total); in Row 9, these sts are decreased across the row.*

Row 1 (right side): K2; *YO, K1; (P1, K1) 7 times; YO, K1; rep from * across, ending last rep with K2 instead of K1: 165 sts.

Row 2: K3; *(P1, K1) 7 times; P1, K3; rep from * across.

Row 3: K3; *YO, K1; (P1, K1) 7 times; YO, K3; rep from * across: 183 sts.

Row 4: K4; *(P1, K1) 7 times; P1, K5; rep from * across, ending last rep with K4.

Row 5: K4; *YO, K1; (P1, K1) 7 times; YO, K5; rep from * across, ending last rep with K4: 201 sts.

Instructions continued on page 18

Row 6: K5; *(P1, K1) 7 times; P1, K7; rep from * across, ending last rep with K5.

Row 7: K5; *YO, K1; (P1, K1) 7 times; YO, K7; rep from *, across ending last rep with K5: 219 sts.

Row 8: K6; *(P1, K1) 7 times; P1, K9; rep from * across, ending last rep with K6.

Row 9: K6; *(sl 1 as to knit, K1, PSSO) 3 times; sl 1 as to knit, K2tog, PSSO; (K2tog) 3 times; K9; rep from * across ending last rep with K6: 147 sts (72 sts decreased).

Row 10: Purl across.

Repeat Rows 1 through 10 until piece measures about 60" (152 cm). BO; weave in all ends.

Textured Arrowheads

Skill Level: Intermediate

Bulky weight yarn and large needles combine to make this afghan with its flowing lines and interesting texture a very special coverlet.

Size
Approximately 48" x 60" (122 cm x 152 cm)

Materials
Bulky weight yarn

[80% acrylic, 20% nylon, 3 ounces, 155 yards (85 grams, 141 meters) per ball]

    8 balls rose

Note: *Photographed model made with Caron® Dazzleaire #0001 Summer Rose*

36" Size 13 (9 mm) circular knitting needle (or size required for gauge)

Gauge
10 sts = 4" (10 cm) in stockinette st (knit 1 row, purl 1 row)

Stitch Guide
BB (Bobble): In next st, work (K1, P1) twice; turn, P4. Pass 2nd, 3rd and 4th sts one at a time over first st, turn. Knit into back of this st: BB made.

Instructions
CO 133 sts. Do not join; work back and forth in rows.

Knit 2 rows.

Instructions continued on page 20.

Row 1: K8; *P4, K5, P4; rep from * to last 8 sts, K8.

Row 2: K7, P1; *K4, P5, K4; rep from * to last 8 sts, P1, K7.

Row 3: K8; *P3, K2tog, K1, (YO, K1) twice; K2tog tbl, P3; rep from to last 8 sts, K8.

Row 4: K7, P1; *K3; P7, K3; rep from * to last 8 ts, P1, K7.

Row 5: K8; *P2, K2tog, K1, YO, K3, YO, K1, K2tog tbl, P2; rep from * to last 8 sts, K8.

Row 6: K7, P1; *K2, P9, K2; rep from * to last 8 sts, P1, K7.

Row 7: K8; *P1, K2tog, K1, YO, K5, YO, K1, K2tog tbl; P1; rep from * to last 8 sts, K8.

Row 8: K7, P1; *K1, P11, K1; rep from * to last 8 sts, P1, K7.

Row 9: K8; *K2tog; K1, YO, K3, BB, K3, YO, K1, K2tog tbl; rep from * to last 8 sts, K8.

Row 10: K7, purl to last 7 sts, K7.

Row 11: K8; *P4, K5, P4; rep from * to last 8 sts, K8.

Row 12: K7, P1; *K4, P5, K4; rep from * to last 8 sts, P1, K7.

Row 13: K8; *P3, K2tog, K1, (YO, K1) twice; K2tog tbl, P3; rep from * to last 8 sts, K8.

Row 14: K7, P1; *K3, P7, K3; rep from * to last 8 ts, P1, K7.

Row 15: K8; *P2, K2tog, K1, YO, K3, YO, K1, K2tog tbl, P2; rep from * to last 8 sts, K8.

Row 16: K7, P1; *K2, P9, K2; rep from * to last 8 sts, P1, K7.

Row 17: K8; *P1, K2tog, K1, YO, K5, YO, K1, K2tog tbl; P1; rep from * to last 8 sts, K8.

Row 18: K7, P1; *K1, P11, K1; rep from * to last 8 sts, P1, K7.

Row 19: K8; *K2tog; K1, YO, K3, BB, K3, YO, K1, K2tog tbl; rep from * to last 8 sts, K8.

Row 20: K7, purl to last 7 sts, K7.

Rep Rows 1 through 20 untl afghan measures approximately 60" (122 cm) from CO edge.

Knit 2 rows. BO; weave in all ends.

Festive Tweed

Skill Level: Intermediate

Bulky yarns work up quickly and easily so you can knit an attractive accent for your home in no time. By knitting with two different colors in the textured stitch used here you can make not only a beautiful afghan, but a touchable one as well.

Size

Approximately 44" x 56" (112 cm x 142 cm)

Materials

Bulky Weight yarn

[100% acrylic, 3.5 ounces, 138 yards (100 grams, 126 meters) per skein]

    9 balls red (color A)

    7 balls grey (Color B)

Note: *Photographed model made with Red Heart® Chunky™ #7252 Fire (Color A) and #7857 Coastal (Color B)*

36" size 11" (8 mm) circular knitting needle (or size required for gauge)

Gauge

14 sts = 4" (10 cm) in stockinette st (knit 1 row, purl 1 row)

Stitch Guide

Cluster (CL): P3tog, keeping 3 purl sts on left-hand needle and transferring new stitch onto right-hand needle, YO, purl same 3 sts tog: 3 sts.

Instructions

With Color A, CO 159 sts; do not join; work back and forth in rows. Carry unused color loosely along the side.

Instructions continued on page 24.

Row 1 (right side): With Color A, knit across.

Row 2: With Color A, K1, P1; *CL, P1; rep from * to last st, K1.

Row 3: Join Color B, knit across.

Row 4: With Color B, K1, P3, CL; *P1, CL; rep from * to last 4 sts, P3, K1.

Rep Rows 1 through 4 until afghan measures approximatly 56" (142 cm), ending by working Row 4.

Last Row: With Color A, knit across.

BO loosely; weave in all ends.

Fringe

Follow Single Knot Fringe instructions on page 31. Using color A, cut strands 16" long, and use 2 strands doubled for each knot. Tie knot in every other stitch on the short ends of the afghan.

GARTER GREATNESS
Skill Level: Easy

Here is an afghan made with the easiest of all knitting: just rows of garter stitch. Yet the result is a spectacular creation combining two contrasting but complimentary yarns. The entire afghan is worked with four strands of yarn, two of one color and two of the other on a large circular needle. The end result is an afghan that is perfect for the extra warmth needed by the sports fan at the stadium.

Size
Approximately 44" x 60" (112 cm x 152 cm)

Materials
Worsted Weight yarn

[100% acrylic, 7 ounces, 364 yards (198 grams, 333 meters) per skein]

    6 skeins purple (Color A)

[100% acrylic, 3.5 ounces, 190 yards (100 grams, 174 meters) per skein]

    12 skeins blue (Color B)

Note: *Photographed model made with Red Heart® Super Saver® #528 medium purple and Red Heart® Classic™ #818 Blue Jewel*

36" size 15 (10 mm) circular knitting needle (or size required for gauge)

Gauge
10 sts = 6" (15 cm) in garter stitch with four strands in garter stitch (knit each row)

Instructions continued on page 27

Instructions

With two strands of color A and two strands of color B, CO 70 sts; do not join. Work back and forth in rows.

Row 1: Knit across.

Row 2: Knit across.

Repeat Rows 1 and 2 until the afghan measures 60" (152 cm). BO all sts; weave in all ends.

GENERAL DIRECTIONS

Abbreviations and Symbols

Knit patterns are written in a special shorthand, which is used so that instructions don't take up too much space. They sometimes seem confusing, but once you learn them, you'll have no trouble following them.

These are Standard Abbreviations

BB	bobble
Beg	beginning
BO	bind off
CL	cluster
Cm	centimeter
CO	cast on
Cont	continue
Inc	increase(ing)
K	knit
K2tog	knit two stitches together
Lp(s)	loop(s)
Lpst	loop stitch
Mm	millimeter(s)
Oz	ounces
P	purl
P2tog	purl two stitches together
Patt	pattern
Prev	previous
PSSO	pass the slipped stitch over
Rem	remain(ing)
Rep	repeat(ing)
Rnd	round
Sl	slip
St(s)	stitch(es)
Tbl	through back loop
Tog	together
YB	yarn in back of needle
YF	yarn in front of needle
YO	Yarn over the needle
YRN	Yarn around needle

These are Standard Symbols

*An asterisk (or double asterisks**) in a pattern row, indicates a portion of instructions to be used more than once. For instance, "rep from * three times" means that after working the instructions once, you must work them again three times for a total of 4 times in all.

† A dagger (or double daggers ††) indicates that those instructions will be repeated again later in the same row or round.

: The number after a colon tells you the number of stitches you will have when you have completed the row or round.

( ) Parentheses enclose instructions which are to be worked the number of times following the parentheses. For instance, "(K1, P2) 3 times" means that you knit one stitch and then purl two stitches, three times.

Parentheses often set off or clarify a group of stitches to be worked into the same space or stitch.

[ ] Brackets and ( ) parentheses are also used to give you additional information. For instance, "(rem sts are left unworked)"

Terms

Finish off—This means to end your piece by pulling the yarn end through the last loop remaining on the needle. This will prevent the work from unraveling.

Continue in Pattern as Established—This means to follow the pattern stitch as if has been set up, working any increases or decreases in such a way that the pattern remains the same as it was established.

Work even—This means that the work is continued in the pattern as established without increasing or decreasing.

Gauge

This is probably the most important aspect of knitting!

Gauge simply means the number of stitches per inch that result from a specified yarn worked with needles in a specified size. But since everyone knits differently —some loosely, some tightly, some in-between—the measurements of individual work can vary greatly, even when the knitters use the same pattern and the same size yarn and or needle.

If you don't work to the gauge specified in the pattern, your project will never be the correct size, and you may not have enough yarn to finish your project. Needle sizes given in instructions are merely guides, and should never be used without a gauge swatch.

To make a gauge swatch, knit a swatch that is about 4" square, using the suggested needle and the number of stitches given in the pattern. Measure your swatch. If the number of stitches is fewer than those listed in the pattern, try making another swatch with a smaller needle. If the number of stitches is more than is called for in the pattern, try making another swatch with a larger needle. It is your responsibility to make sure you achieve the gauge specified in the pattern.

Knitting Needles

Knitting needles in the United States are usually marked with numbers. In most of the rest of the world, knitting needles are indicated with metrics. Here is a guide from the Craft Yarn Council:

US Number	Metric
0	2 mm
1	2.25 mm
2	2.75 mm
3	3.25 mm
4	3.5 mm
5	3.75 mm
6	4 mm
7	4.5 mm
8	5 mm
9	5.5 mm
10	6 mm
$10^{1/2}$	6.5 mm
11	8 mm
13	9 mm
15	10 mm
17	12.75 mm
19	15 mm
50	25 mm

Knit Terminology

The patterns in this book have been written using the knitting terminology that is used in the United States. Terms which may have different equivalents in other parts of the world are listed below.

United States	International
Gauge	Tension
Skip	Miss
Yarn over (YO)	Yarn forward (yfwd)
Bind off	Cast off

Standard Yarn Weights

To make it easier for yarn manufacturers, publishers, and designers to prepare consumer-friendly products and for consumers to select the right materials for a project, the following standard yarn weight system has been adopted.

Standard Yarn Weight System
Categories of yarn, gauge, ranges, and recommended needle and hook sizes

Yarn Weight Symbol & Category	0 Lace	1 Super Fine	2 Fine	3 Light	4 Medium	5 Bulky	6 Super Bulky
Type of Yarns in Category	Fingering 10 count crochet	Sock, Fingering, Baby	Sport, Baby	DK, Light, Worsted	Worsted, Afghan, Aran	Chunky, Craft, Rug	Bulky, Roving
Knit Gauge Range* in Stockinette Stitch to 4 inches	33-40** sts	27-32 sts	23-26 sts	21-24 sts	16-20 sts	12-15 sts	6-11 sts
Recommended Needle in Metric Size Range	1.5-2.25 mm	2.25-3.25mm	3.25-3.75mm	3.75-4.5mm	4.5-5.5mm	5.5-8mm	8mm and larger
Recommended Needle U.S. Size Range	000-1	1 to 3	3 to 5	5 to 7	7 to 9	9 to 11	11 and larger

* GUIDELINES ONLY: The above reflect the most commonly used gauges and needle or hook sizes for specific yarn categories.

** Lace weight yarns are usually knitted or crocheted on larger needles and hooks to create lacy, openwork patterns. Accordingly, a gauge range is difficult to determine. Always follow the gauge stated in your pattern.

Skill Levels

Yarn manufacturers, publishers, needle and hook manufacturers have worked together to set up a series of guidelines and symbols to bring uniformity to patterns. Before beginning a project, check to see if your skill level is equal to the one listed for the project.

- **Beginner** — Projects for first-time knitters using basic knit and purl stitches. Minimal shaping.
- **Easy** — Projects using basic stitches, repetitive stitch patterns, simple color changes, and simple shaping and finishing.
- **Intermediate** — Projects with a variety of stitches, such as basic cables and lace, simple intarsia, double-pointed needles and knitting in the round needle techniques, mid-level shaping and finishing.
- **Experienced** — Projects using advanced techniques and stitches, such as short rows, fair isle, more intricate intarsia, cables, lace patterns, and numerous color changes.

Fringe

Basic Instructions

Cut a piece of cardboard about 6" wide and half as long as specified in the instructions for strands, plus ½" for trimming allowance. Wind the yarn loosely and evenly lengthwise around the cardboard. When the card is filled, cut the yarn across one end. Do this several times; then begin fringing. You can wind additional strands as you need them.

Single Knot Fringe

Hold the specified number of strands for one knot of fringe together, then fold in half.

Hold the project with the right side facing you. Using a crochet hook, draw the folded ends through the space or stitch from right to wrong side.

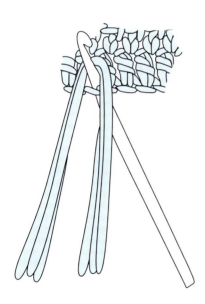

Pull the loose ends through the folded section,

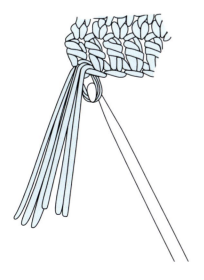

Draw the knot up firmly.

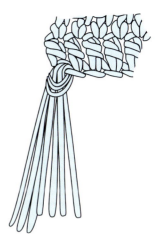

Space the knots evenly and trim the ends of the fringe.

Double Knot Fringe

Begin by working Single Knot Fringe. With right side facing you and working from left to right, take half the strands of one knot and half the strands in the knot next to it, and knot them together.

Triple Knot Fringe

First work Double Knot Fringe. Then working again on right side from left to right, tie the third row of knots.

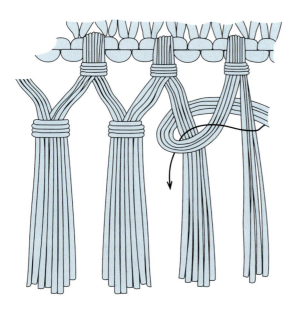
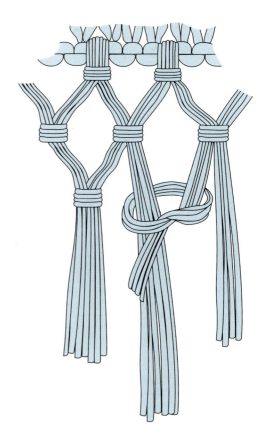